I0439349

Dinosaur Coloring Book For Kids

Dinosaur Coloring Book inlcuding Tyrannosaurus Rex, Velociraptor, Triceratops and many more.

Coloring Books For Kids: Vol 1

by The Coloring Book People

ISBN-13: 978-1534955660

ISBN-10: 1534955666

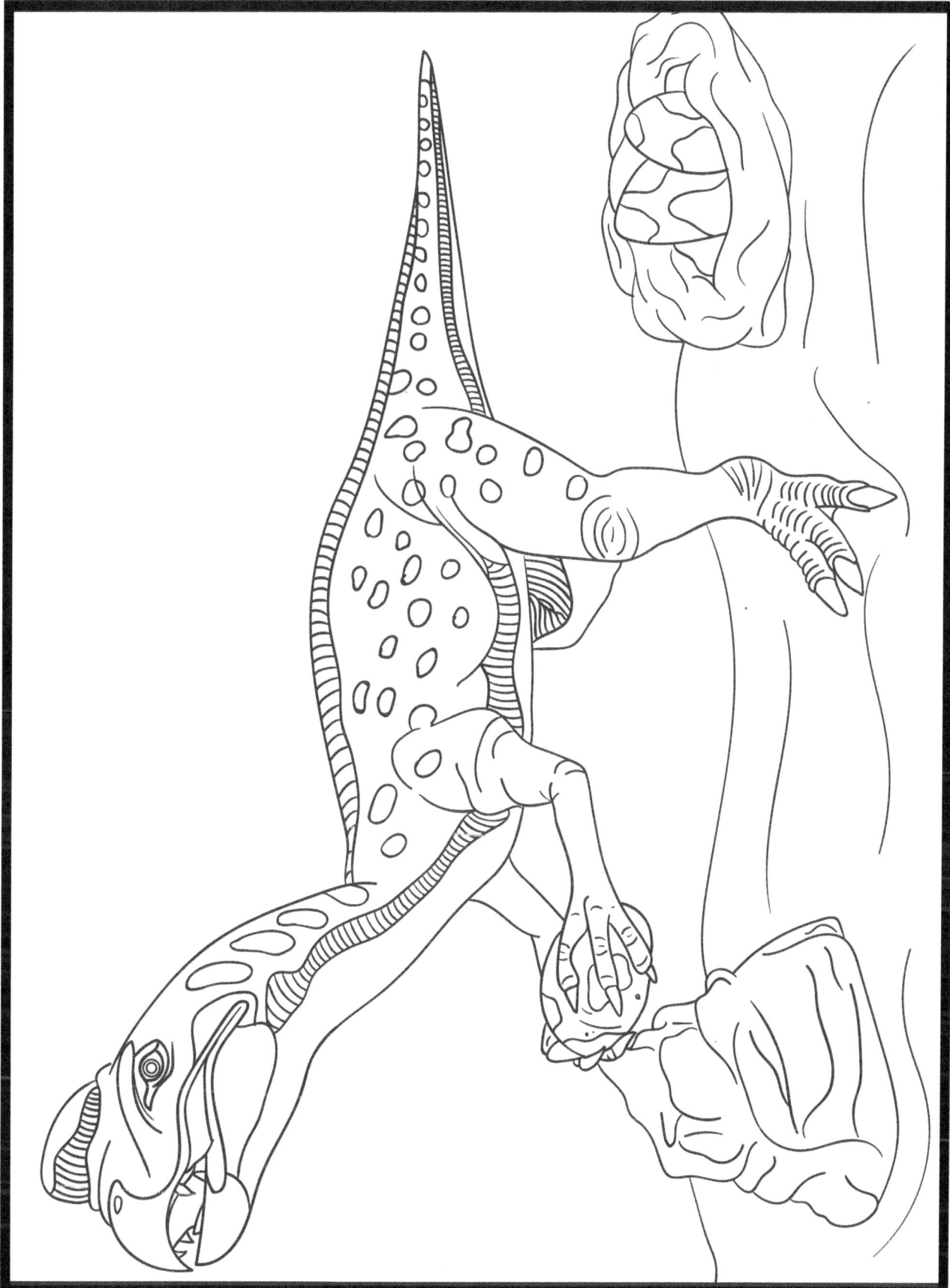

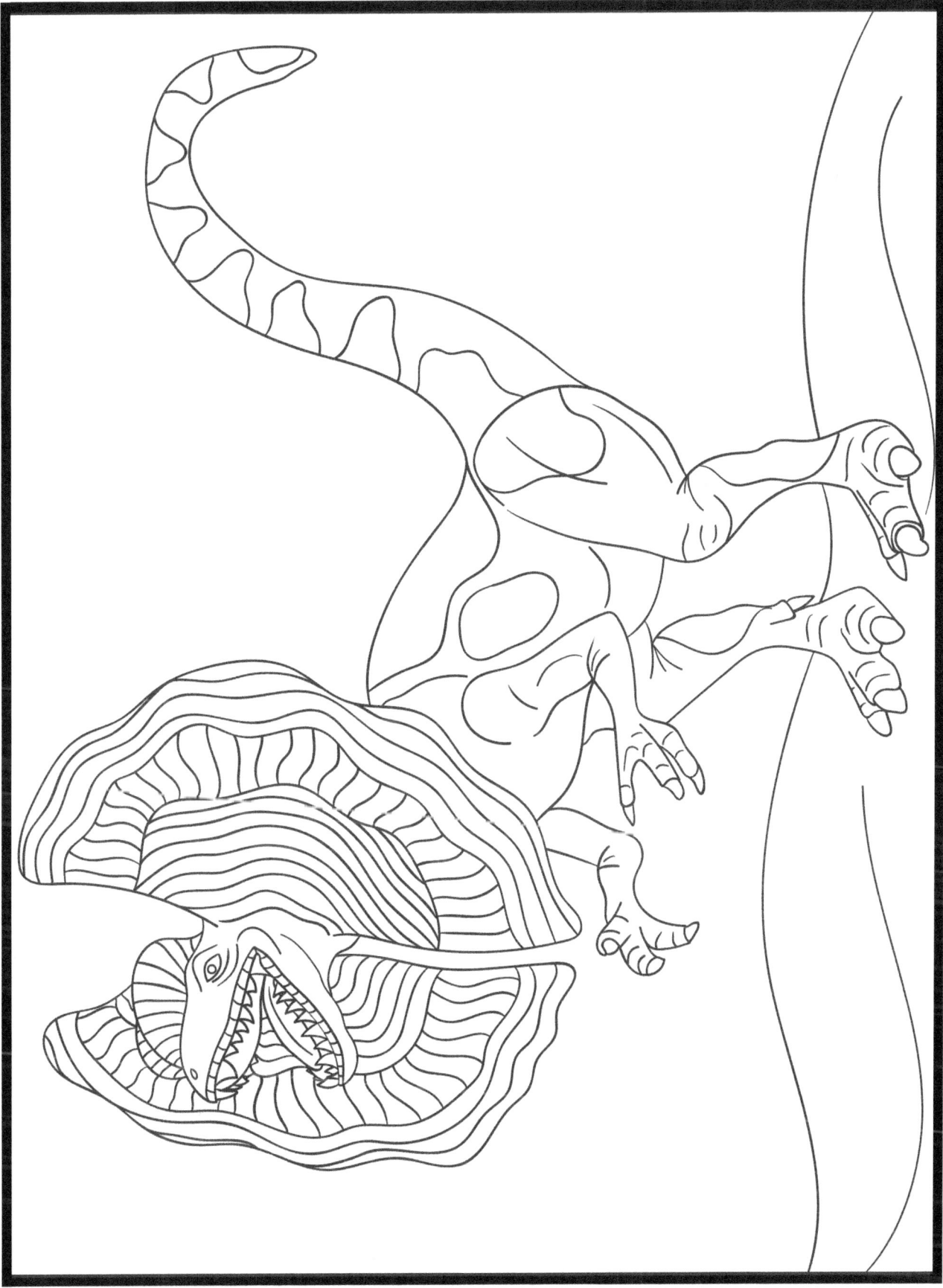

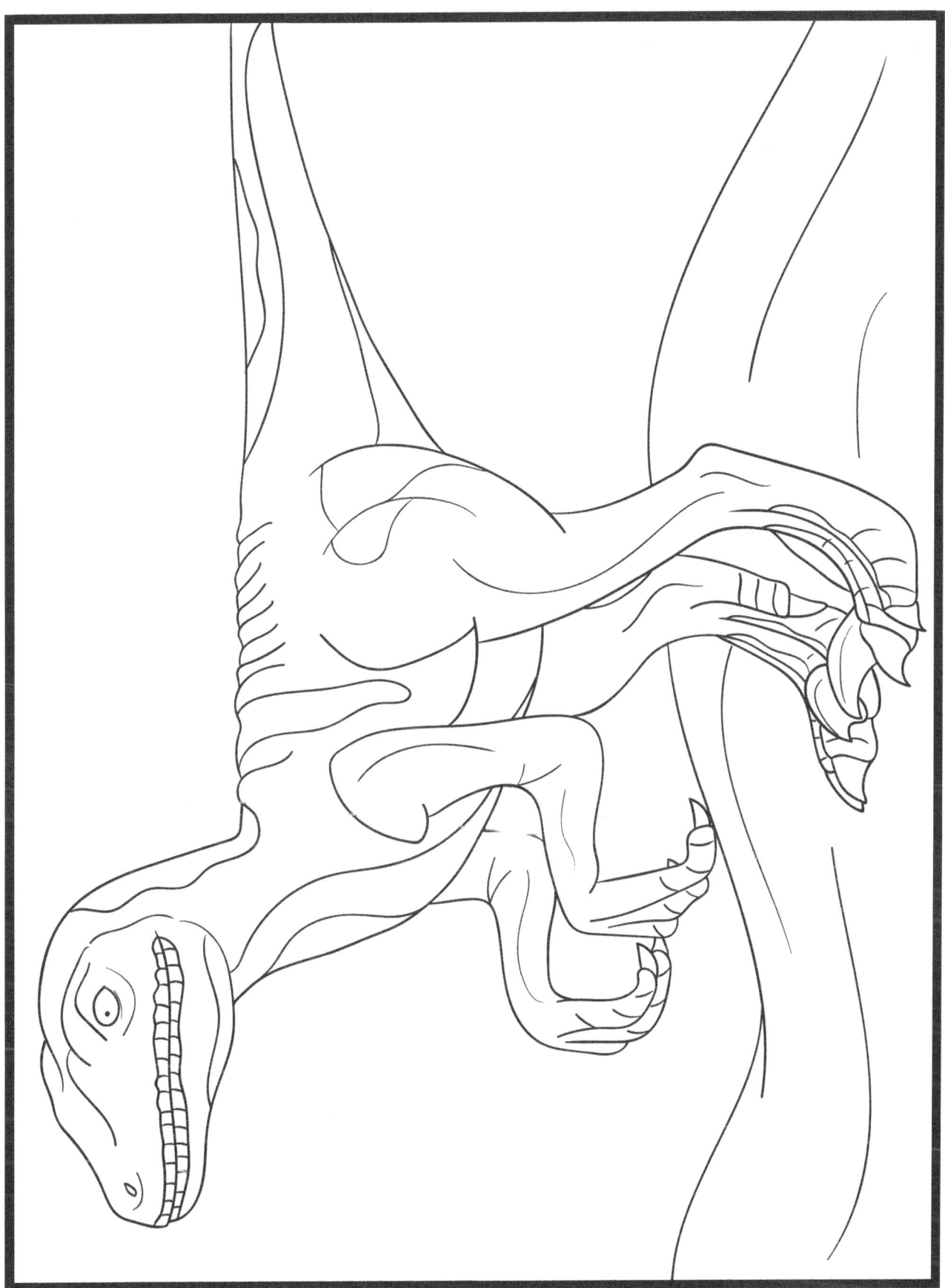

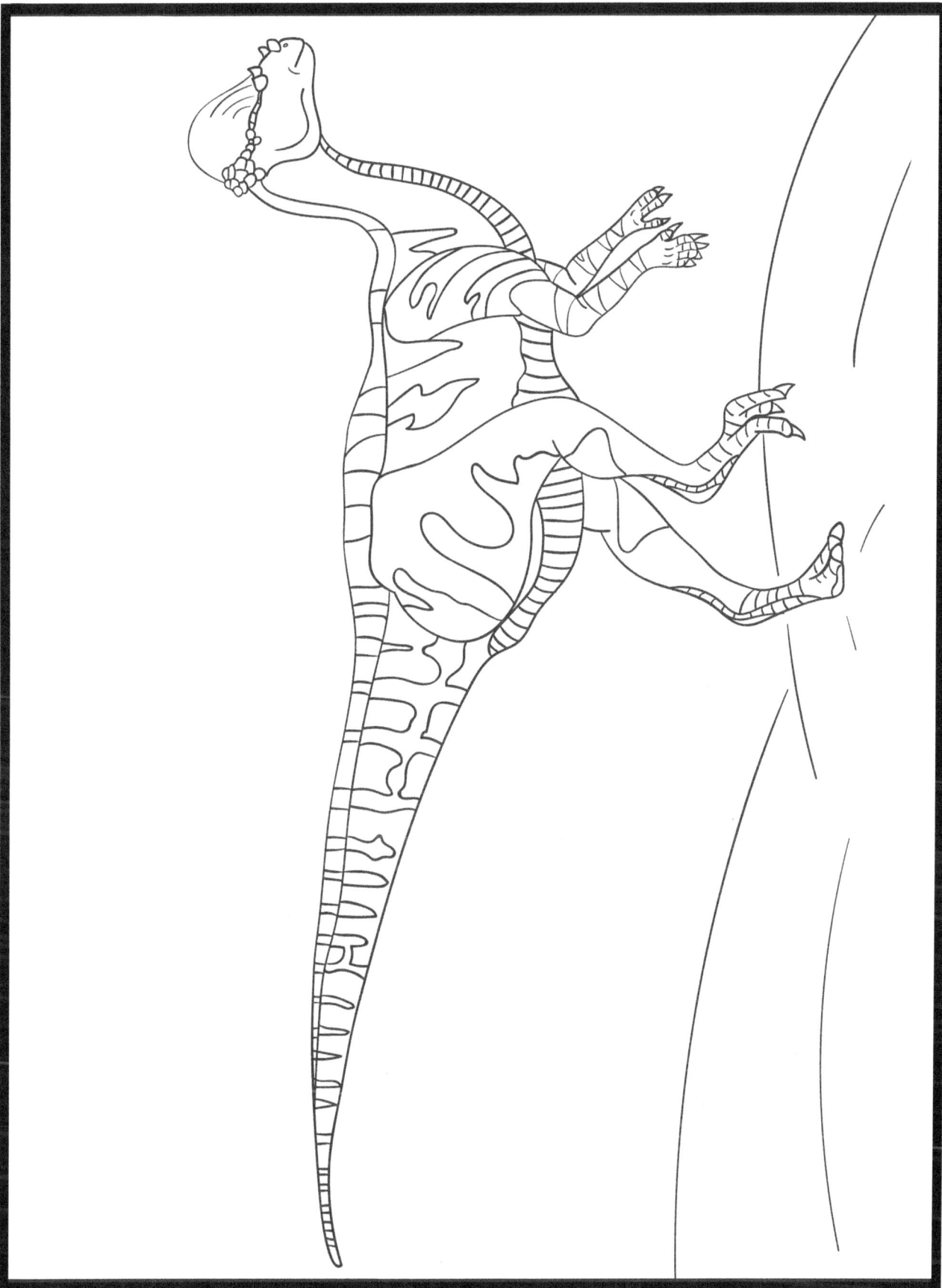

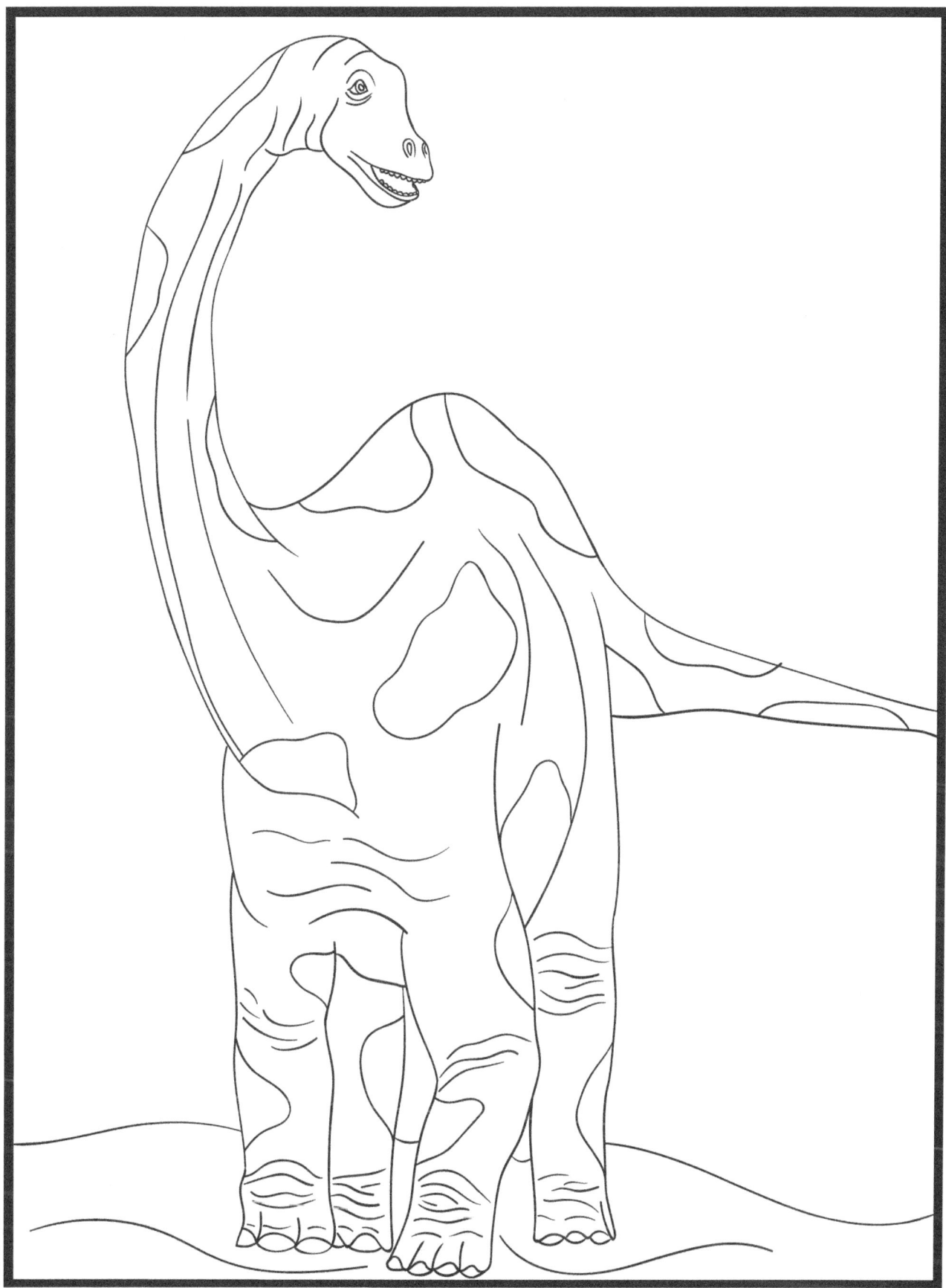